It's Time to P.O.P. Prosper on Purpose

Anastasia Means Dallas

It's Time to P.O.P. Prosper on Purpose
Copyright © 2018 by Anastasia Means Dallas All Rights Reserved.

All rights reserved. No part of this book may be reproduced in any form or by any electronic or mechanical means including information storage and retrieval systems, without permission in writing from the author. The only exception is by a reviewer, who may quote short excerpts in a review.

Printed in the United States of America

First Printing: Aug 2018

ISBN-9781718019188

from author of Amazon Best Seller,

 **THE 7 PRINCIPLES OF SUCCESS**

THE 7 CONCEPTS OF CUSTOMER SERVICE

How to Win Over Your Customers and Keep Them Coming Back!

A Short and Practical Guide for Companies and Employees to Raise Standards of Customer Service.

Joshua S. Kangley

The 7 Concepts of Customer Service:

How to Win Over Your Customers and Keep Them Coming Back!

A Short and Practical Guide for Companies and Employees to Raise Standards of Customer Service

By Joshua Kangley

To my husband,
Roy Dallas Jr., you are the best musician I know. Thank you for your support in every project that I've ever taken, that means the world to me.

To my son,
Cameron Austin, I am very proud of the man that God is molding you into, just know you are equally gifted in this writing space.

To my son,
Jalen Bryant, you are intelligent, and you've always had wisdom beyond your years, I can't wait to see how God is going to use you for his kingdom.

To my son,
Zachary Ryan, you are one of the most humorous people I know, and one day you will make your mark on the world with all your gifts and talents.

To my mom & dad,
Deborah Bowman Lightfoot & Willie J. Means, I pray that I am in line with scripture when it says to honor thy mother and father and that your days may be long on the earth. I love you!

To my grandma,
Alice Stringfellow, you have not missed a beat! Your laugh is contagious, and your love for me is undeniable.

Special Thanks:
To my family and friends for their support throughout the years.

Table of Contents

Introduction 1
Chapter 1: It Was His Will from the Beginning 2
Chapter 2: Stuck Between A Rock and A Hard Place 7
Chapter 3: The Spirit of Mammon 10
Chapter 4: The Struggle Was Real 12
Chapter 5: Money Matters - The Kingdom Mindset 20
Chapter 6: Money with A Purpose 23

7 Keys to P.O.P. (Prosper on Purpose) 26
Chapter 7: Key #1 See God as Your Only Source 27
Chapter 8: Key #2 Renew Your Mind 32
Chapter 9: Key #3 See Your Job as Your Seed 36
Chapter 10: Key #4 Begin Speaking Life 40
Chapter 11: Key #5 Increase Your Financial I.Q. 44
Chapter 12: Key #6 Teach Your Children the Language of Wealth 49
Chapter 13: Key #7 Begin Empowering Others 55
About the Author 60

INTRODUCTION

We've heard this scripture in church, we've read it for ourselves, or we've heard someone quote: "Beloved, I pray that you may prosper in all things and be in health, just as your soul prospers." (3 John 1:2). For some it has taken on the meaning of money only, and some people have associated it with health only, but the conclusion of the matter is this: the Merriam-Webster Dictionary defines the word *prosper* as: (1) to succeed in an enterprise or activity, especially to achieve economic success; (2) to become strong and flourishing. The King James Version Dictionary defines it as: (1) to favor, to render successful; (2) To be successful, to succeed; (3) To grow or increase; to thrive; to make gain.

From what I've gathered from the definitions of both sources, to prosper means there's nothing missing, lacking, or broken in any area of our lives: finances, health, relationships. In other words, we're moving from glory to glory. I don't think God stuttered when he said that above all things he wants us to prosper and be in good health even as our soul prospers. This has always been his desire for his children. The paramount question then becomes, why aren't we experiencing this in every area of our lives if God wills this for us? Could it be that we don't think we deserve it?

For years I felt like I didn't deserve to be blessed or prosper because of the many mistakes I'd made in my past. This is a dangerous way of thinking because if you don't believe that you are supposed to have something, don't worry, you won't have it. One sign of believing in something is that we begin to speak it. Most people don't go around talking about something they really don't believe in.

CHAPTER 1: IT WAS HIS WILL FROM THE BEGINNING

When you believe in something, and you're confident about it, you want the whole world to know about it. How many times have you found a good product or a restaurant, and it exceeded your expectations? Most likely you told everyone you knew that could benefit from it. Could it be that we haven't been exposed to this as being the will of God for our lives? The word of God is the will of God, so if we don't read, or know what's in the bible, it's pretty much impossible to follow what it says. Could it be that it hasn't been taught? Coming from a single mom I witnessed my mom working hard. Sometimes I've witnessed her working more than one job to ensure that our needs were met. We never discussed finances, and a lot of times we were surrounded by people who were always struggling and begging and trying to make a dollar out of fifteen cents. All the people in my neighborhood knew that my mom was a giver, whether it was money, flour, milk, or God knows whatever. This is just the way it was living in the projects in the 70's back then. My mom still has a heart of gold to this day. Your environment is also a contributor to your thinking and your belief system.

I saw my grandfather run a successful shoe shop business when I was in elementary school, but of course I didn't associate him as being an entrepreneur and using his gifts to support his family. His gift as a cobbler was making room for him. All of this was biblical, but I had no clue because I wasn't exposed to the promises in the bible because we only attended church on Christmas, New Year's, and Easter. I didn't discover until later why we didn't attend church regularly. Unfortunately, my Mom didn't have a great respect for preachers, and rightfully so because of what she told me. Although I didn't necessarily grow up in the church, when I did decide to go, I joined a Baptist church and I was baptized at eighteen. I learned a lot of things about how to live right and stay of the clubs, and how to praise God, but I didn't learn much about what God expected of me except for giving my tithes and offerings. This was even taught from the point of view which is a part of the Mosaic law: if you don't give, don't expect to be blessed, or God is going to get you. It was always from a position of fear and we already know that God has not given us the spirit of fear, but of power, love, and a sound mind.

My Pastor was very comical at the time, and he would always joke about people falling down the stairs or having a flat tire because they didn't pay their tithes. He was joking, but serious at the same time. My Pastor most likely only taught what he knew or understood at the time. A lot of churches, especially the African American churches, were using fear to get people to give because they didn't trust God would make provision for their vision. Things haven't changed much because there are some people who are afraid to give, fearing that they won't have enough left to meet their needs. What ends up happening, is you manifest what you believe. There were some people who suffered loss, not because God was getting them back for not tithing, but they believed that he was punishing them.

I remember in the book of Job when he was going through all his trials, and he wasn't getting sound advice even from the people he loved and trusted the most. I hear people misinterpreting what happened to Job all the time, and they have the nerve to say this famous scripture at most homegoing services, "The Lord giveth, and the Lord taketh away, blessed be the name of the Lord." They omit the scripture that tells what really happened to Job which was the thing that Job feared the most came upon him. You see, faith can work both ways, whatever you put your faith in will manifest.

Tithing is an issue of faith and belief. It's a privilege to get to give to God. In fact, we get to give, and by giving we're simply letting God know that he is our only source.

It also shows that we are giving God our best. It isn't different from what happened to Cain and Abel. This was a matter of Abel giving his first and best, while Cain chose to give God the leftovers. His jealousy arose eventually leading him to kill his own brother. When we operate with a kingdom mindset, we understand quickly that God is not broke, and he doesn't need our money. He just needs an avenue for us to show that we trust him, and money is one of the ways that we can do this. Even in the biblical days when they didn't have physical money, they gave their first and best of whatever they had, whether it was crops or cattle.

Why are so many people who are believers not participating in this awesome opportunity to demonstrate their faith? Could it be perhaps that our mindset and religion has prevented us from walking in freedom and receiving all that God has for us? There were and still are religious folk, and unchurched folk who still believe that Pastors and God's children are supposed to be broke. They give the story of Jesus being born in a manger, and there was nowhere for him to lay his head. I sometimes meet people who claim that the church just wants your money, but so does Burger King, Macy's, BMW, and other retailers. That's not the point, but it's inevitable that you need money to live in this world, and to be able to bless others. We are blessed to be a blessing! I've also heard people say, "Money is the root of all evil," when in fact it says, "The love of money is the root of all evil...." (I Timothy 6:10).

The only evil thing I see is not being able to pay your light bill, mortgage, or buy food for your family. The worst kind of evil is having to raise money to bury our loved ones because we didn't prepare properly, or seeing a family or friend being put out of their home for not being able to pay their rent or mortgage because we can't contribute any money. We can fool ourselves and convince one another that money isn't important, but that would be deception in the highest form. Money is important, and it money does matter.

If money is not important, it wouldn't be mentioned at all in the bible. Part of the scripture declares in Ecclesiastes 10:19, "Money answereth all things." Did you know that the word money is mentioned in the bible 800 times? I'd say that it's important! In fact, if you look at the world, and what's going on in neighborhoods and communities, most of the crimes can be tracked back to a money issue. Think about it, a robber steals something because he doesn't understand that God shall supply all his needs according to his riches and glory in Christ Jesus. People go through rain, sleet, and snow to a job to make money.

IT'S TIME TO P.O.P. PROSPER ON PURPOSE

You're probably not surprised to find that some people don't like their jobs or wish that they could be doing something totally different. We are trading our time to make money, which is fine, but we must consider other ways of making money that would free up our time if that's our ultimate desire. Lawmakers and politicians make policies and laws based on money, sometimes to people's demise. I have found people angry with me because I want a quality life for my family, and I choose not to live in poverty. It can make some people uncomfortable when you have uncommon goals, and unconventional ways to achieve those goals. There are a lot of people that are comfortable with the 8-5, retiring, and perhaps getting a second job. I'm not against working a job especially if you're passionate about it, and you're using it as a vehicle to finance your freedom. It is possible to achieve wealth and Prosper on Purpose, we just must seek God for wisdom. That's why the bible admonishes us that if we lack wisdom, to ask, and he will give it to us liberally. (Paraphrase of James 1:5)

Once we find out where the origin is or the root of the problem, we can move towards a solution. I was able to pinpoint some areas in my life that caused me to not think soberly when it comes to what God willed for my life, and I pray that you're able to locate any area that's preventing you from having God's best in life. I remember visiting this church once that didn't believe in healing. I promise you that half of the congregation was sick, on oxygen, in wheelchairs, or just plain defeated in their bodies. This was evident to me that when people don't understand their kingdom privileges, they succumb to the lies of the enemy.

This book is not just about money, or another get rich scheme type of book, it's a book that shows my personal and up-close journey about how do you Prosper on Purpose, God's way. No matter where you find yourself in life today, there's always hope. I've read books about people who have reached multi-millionaire status and wholeness in their life, but you rarely read about people who are in the process. The bible is and always will be our final authority and our road map for this life. In fact, we overcome by the blood of the lamb and by the word of our testimony. (Revelation 12:11). I consider myself in the process, and hopefully this book will allow you to move into a place where you can discover keys consequently that you can begin or continue to P.O.P. (Prosper on Purpose). It is the will of God to prosper you and that you be in good health even as your soul prospers.

CHAPTER 2: STUCK BETWEEN A ROCK AND A HARD PLACE

The area of finances is an area where I feel as though I have experienced the least amount of victory in my life. I did everything that I thought that mounted up to success. I went to college, chose a stable career, and I started operating in some of the gifts that God blessed me with. I didn't lack money because I have always been blessed to have money, but I couldn't save any money. I didn't know anything about investing, and I never even fathomed paying myself first after paying my tithes. There was a big gap between what God promised in his word, and what I was experiencing. I was stuck between a rock and a hard place.

My husband and I both work in the field of education, and we made over six-figure combined incomes but were still drowning in debt. This opened my eyes even more to see that you can make as much money as you will, but if you don't have the proper mindset and wisdom when it comes to money, it will not benefit you at all. We had all the outward appearances that the world considered success: a three-story home, four vehicles, vacations on the fly, and dinner at restaurants on a regular basis. To be honest, I felt that if we gave the ten percent for tithes, the ninety percent was there for us to enjoy until our hearts were content. I didn't realize that money had a mission, and that it repelled people who mismanaged it. I did have a monthly budget, but I didn't follow it, and every dollar was not accounted for.

The sad part about it is that the money we were making still didn't afford us an opportunity to make ends meet. There was usually more month than money, and sometimes we found ourselves going in the red with our bank accounts, borrowing money from family, or just plain going without. We were in fact drowning in debt. The bill collectors were calling, and we were trying to figure out who we could not pay for that month so we could at least keep food on the table. Debt had gripped us, and we were sinking. The financial tension caused a strain on our marriage of course because we were always uptight, wondering what our next move would be.

How can two totally educated Christians find themselves in this position as tithers' people may ask? Easy. We hadn't made Jesus lord over our finances, and both of us had a poverty mindset. On the outside it appeared that we were winning, when we were actually losing.

The spirit of mammon was in full gear, along with the spirit of materialism. The spirit of mammon is operating on the earth today, and people don't realize that they are actual victims of it. The spirit of mammon comes in when you look to everything but God to meet your needs, and not acknowledge him as your only source. The spirit of mammon is scared to give because it has you thinking that if you give anything away, you won't have enough for yourself. Then to top it off, the spirit of materialism doesn't help at all. The spirit of materialism is always wanting more, and usually for the wrong reasons.

We were already living in a three-story home, but desired to move in a gated community. We were already driving an Infiniti Q 56, but desired to drive a Bentley. Don't get me wrong, there isn't anything wrong with having any of things that I've mentioned above, but you must be positioned to buy it, and you must have the right motive and mindset. Have you ever seen people who win the lottery, or inherit a large sum of money, and the next year or two, they are totally broke? That's what happens when you obtain things and your mind has not been renewed, and you lack the wisdom to handle it.

The transparency revealed in this book is designed to help others who have fallen prey to this, and they're looking for a way out. If the cycle is not broken, we can find ourselves passing this type of living on to our kids. Like us, so many people have bought the lie that it's ok to accumulate debt and live above your means. When we're in debt we become servant to the lenders, much like slavery. You feel the bondage that you are in, and you long to be free.

Today you see more and more people relying on GoFundMe to help bury their loved ones, and instead of leaving an inheritance, people are starting to leave their children debt. Let's work toward leaving a legacy for our family by being intentional with our finances and learning how to prosper on purpose. For us to receive healing in our finances, we must identify how we got where we are, so we can begin moving forward.

CHAPTER 3: THE SPIRIT OF MAMMON

I really didn't understand the spirit of mammon until recently when I heard my Pastor, Dr. Creflo Dollar, conduct a series on it. The spirit of mammon is attached to money, and it is running rampantly in the world today. The spirit of mammon is to trust money more than God. If we aren't aware of the spirit of mammon, we can operate in it by default. I will direct you to a scripture that I've always heard, but it brings what I'm talking about to life. "No man can serve two masters: for either he will hate the one and love the other; or else he will hold to the one and despise the other. Ye cannot serve God and mammon."

This scripture hit me like a bolt of lightning because it's telling me that if my relationship with money is that of a servant and master, and money is my master, I hate God. That's a very strong statement but it's true. Look at how a borrower can be the servant to the lender. "The rich rule over the poor, and the borrower is servant to the lender." (Proverbs 22:7). There have been times when I had to borrow money to buy a house, car, and to pay for my college education. The only problem with this is that we've been taught that being in debt is not a problem, and buying a home is labeled as an asset when it's a liability if it's not paid in cash. If I am having to work more than one job to maintain my standard of living, then that's a good indication that I am being controlled by the spirit of mammon. If I have several credit cards, and the credit card companies are calling me at home, on my job, and disguising their number, that's an indication that I may be operating under the spirit of mammon.

The spirit of mammon also has a spiral effect. If I am having to work more than one job to maintain my standard of living, then that means I'm away from my family, and there's a possibility that my marriage and my children may suffer as a result. That's why this spirit is subtle because you become a victim before you know it.

This spirit is dangerous because it also involves fear. Any time we are dealing with fear, we know that it did not come from God. "For God hath not given us the spirit of fear; but of power, of love, and a sound mind." (2 Timothy 1:7) The fear comes in when we are afraid to give in church and refusing to give and help others because of the fear of running out. Speaking of giving, in the scripture when the rich people were giving, there was a widow mite who gave mites, but God considered her to have given the most. "For all these out of their abundance have put in offerings for God, but she out of her poverty put in all the livelihood that she had." Luke 21:4.

Giving isn't a matter of how much you give, but it's a matter of trust. Do we really trust God? Money has been made the greatest thing, but in the kingdom of God it's considered the least. I have been guilty of mismanaging money and operating in the spirit of mammon. I tithe but there have been plenty of times where I have not prayed, or asked God what he wanted me to do with my money. Considering our motives for wanting more money is also important.

Recently I almost fell in the same ditch because I wanted to have this lavish birthday party on this yacht and make it a red-carpet experience. The problem isn't that I couldn't do it, the problem was why did I want this over-the-top party. After searching my heart, I realized that it would be a party that people would talk about for a long time, it would show how I'm living abroad and balling out of control, and it would be an opportunity to share my party on social media and share with people who could care less. I'm not saying that I won't ever celebrate my birthday in a lavish way, but rest assured my motives for wanting the party will be pure.

I have lived most of my life in a selfish manner not considering the needs of others. There are times when my family has suffered from my seeking fame and fortune, it's just the truth. I'm so glad that I was able to recognize all of this and repent and get in the will of God. I'm no longer living my life to become a multi-millionaire and to become famous. Today I'm living my life to make the name of Jesus famous. Mammon no longer has a place in my life because I have gained understanding in this area.

"Wisdom is the principal thing; Therefore, get wisdom, and in all your getting, get understanding." Proverbs 4:7

CHAPTER 4: THE STRUGGLE WAS REAL

There are two time periods in my life that I will capture in this chapter, the first part dealing with my younger years, and the second part deals with my life as an adult. Your childhood truly does shape your belief system and your life until you have what I call, "THE ENCOUNTER."

I was born in the 1970's in Hartford, Connecticut, during the time President Richard Nixon was president. There was inflation, the stock market was in trouble, economic growth wasn't strong, and unemployment was on the rise. The welfare reform that had been implemented by President Franklin D. Roosevelt was in full effect. The average income per year was about $12,900, the average cost of a new home was $32,500, a gallon of gas was .40 cents and the price of a new car was around $2,900. The cost of living was much higher in the North than it was in the South, and still holds true to this day.

My mom and dad were pretty much a newlywed couple with two small children. My dad worked at a bank, and my mom stayed home for the most part caring for my sister and me. They didn't really struggle because my dad's mom helped them financially, so we were never without. My dad later joined the military and began traveling abroad leaving us behind. This of course eventually put a strain on my parents' marriage with the long-distance relationship, and finally it led to a separation. My mom moved back to the South with her parents, and eventually found herself raising us as a single parent. Having no money and no job, her parents' home was a haven for her, and she knew that not only could she get the support of her parents, but her younger siblings were also there to aid her with my sister and me.

My grandfather was a cobbler, and he operated a very successful shoe business where he repaired shoes, purses, leather coats, just about anything. Of course, at that age I couldn't process the fact that my granddad was an entrepreneur. Not only was he an entrepreneur and my grandmother worked outside of the home at the State Mental Hospital, they never had to depend on government assistance although they reared ten kids. I didn't realize how amazing that was until I got older. There wasn't any lack in my grandparent's home, in fact on most days I would watch him work in the shop and witness the exchange of goods and services. My grandfather kept money in his pocket and hidden in special places in the house. He paid the insurance guy regularly when he stopped by, and he always managed to give me money each day after school so that I could go to the neighborhood store, or swim at the local pool during the summer time. Although we only ate out during special occasions, we always had food, and everything that we needed.

My mom finally decided it was time to find a place of her own. By this time, mom was working and receiving an allotment check from dad who was still in the Army. Life somehow began to change after moving from under my grandparents' roof. We moved to the local projects not far away from my grandparents' home, and I could tell my mom felt a sense of pride about having her own place. It was a two-bedroom, one bath apartment, and it was very clean. My sister and I shared a bedroom, and we had twin beds and matching Raggedy Ann and Andy comforters and curtains. For me honestly, I think that this is where the poverty mind-set kicked in.

Unfortunately, my mom was one of the few people who went to work on our side of the projects, and who had a vehicle. The neighbors quickly realized that not only did my mother work, she had a strong support system because they witnessed our family dropping off clothing, food, gifts, and a plethora of other things to make our new life comfortable. Eventually, we started getting knocks at our door from people asking to borrow sugar, money, and flour, basically everything but the kitchen sink. This is pretty much the onset of the poverty mind set because it became the new normal.

Here I was going from watching my grandfather as entrepreneur exchange goods in services, to watching people asking for things or borrowing. I don't knock the entire process because there was a sense of community because the neighbors cared for each other's well-being. There was always someone watching you in the community. They were what I called the community reporters. They will scold you, and then turn around and tell my mom anything I did wrong. I didn't see this as a benefit at the time; however, our communities are lacking this time of support today. Even when we moved to the other side of town, it was to a newer housing development they had just built. I saw more working-class families or single mothers who were still struggling. They went to work daily, but the money did not last until the end of the month. There was still a sense of community there, but a lot of times I still witnessed people borrowing money for food, or to make ends meet.

Although our living conditions had changed, and this development did attract a working class of people, there was still a struggle in finances. When we finally left our rural town and moved to what we thought was "the big city," things did get a little better, but we were still living in subsidized housing. I felt the sense of community here as well, and most of the people were working class people, and although there wasn't a lot of borrowing going on, you had the neighborhood thief. He would steal shoes, clothes, food, televisions, so basically whatever you needed, he would get it for you. Looking back in retrospect, I know this wasn't right, but back then it was called survival. Although I didn't take on the crime of stealing, the poverty mindset was there, and I fell into the cycle of living from paycheck to paycheck and borrowing money from time to time in my adulthood.

Before I graduated high school, I automatically knew that I wanted to go to college. I was in a local college outreach program that was federally funded, and they allowed us to stay in the dorms during the summer, provided us with a stipend, and gave us additional educational programs throughout the school year. This was a wonderful program that aided many of my friends and I in making the decision to go to college. I appreciate such programs as Upward Bound because not only did they demonstrate to us that college was attainable, they took us to college campuses as well to provide exposure. When we went on the college tour to Atlanta, Georgia, I was certain the Spelman College would be my college of choice, until reality set in and I realized that my mom couldn't afford the tuition.

IT'S TIME TO P.O.P. PROSPER ON PURPOSE

Upon graduating from high school, I graciously accepted grants and attended Florida A & M University, the local HBCU. It all worked out even though I had a couple of detours along the way. I got caught up in credit card debt trying to be like the Jones'. After my classes were paid for, I would go on a massive shopping spree, rent cars, have house parties, and of course get my hair and nails done. Not only had I spent the extra money for my refund check, but when the credit card companies showed up on campus, I readily signed up, and received my free mug. There wasn't anything in me, or training provided that said save your money. I literally spend every dime I received, and graciously waited for the next refund check.

I eventually left college after only being there a year and I decided to join the military. There wasn't anything about me that said that I was military material. Everyone that truly knew me, already understood that the military was not for me especially the Army, the branch I inquired about initially. I wound up joining the Air Force, and I went through basic training, tech school, and then I came home on leave prior to being stationed in Guam. I had never heard of Guam, and I certainly didn't know that it was a U.S. territory.

When I signed up, I was told that there was a great chance that I would remain in my home state of Florida and be stationed at Ft. Walton Beach, of course that didn't happen. So here I was stationed all the way across the world, and after being there only a short period of time, I discovered that I was pregnant. I was young, and I was afraid especially being stationed half around the world away from my support system. I begin to get ill, and finally I decided that I need to request to leave the military and return home.

After going through several processes, I was granted an honorable discharge, and graciously sent back home to be with my family. I'm thankful to this day that they honored my request. I do want to say that the military help me in some areas of my life that I am grateful for even today. I wasn't the most submissive individual in the world, in fact I was very stubborn. The military help to alleviate all of that. Believe it or not, I became a leader in the short time span, I

received an award, and I was promoted. God's favor was on me even when I stepped into something on my own. It reminds of the scripture in Deuteronomy 30:9 when that states that "The Lord will make you successful in everything that you do." I didn't know this scripture personally, and I didn't necessarily have a personal relationship with God. As a matter of fact, I didn't get baptized until I was eighteen years old.
That's just a picture of God's Amazing Grace.

My purpose for going in the military was to serve my country, pay off my debts, and get a free education, at least that's what I told myself. Most of my check went to my phone bill because I was calling home every opportunity that I could. As you can see it didn't make sense for me to leave college in the first place. Now I was having a baby without a college education, and on top of that, I was moving back home with my mom after being out on my own. I hadn't saved any money, so I wasn't in any better shape than before I left. In fact, I had taken on more because now I was becoming a single mother. I had an extremely supportive family, so I didn't have to work during my pregnancy, and after my son was born, my mom rented a massive home for my sister and me and our babies.

By this time, my sister had given birth to her first child, and he was already a year old. My mom has received lawsuits for being injured in accidents, and during this time, she had become an entrepreneur with a Nail Shop with another partner, and she worked full-time for a local state representative. My mom was really prospering at the time. The business was flourishing, and she had money in the bank, and she was able to be a blessing to my sister and me. The money lasted for about two years, and then it was back to living from paycheck to paycheck. My mom and her partner decided to close the nail shop and go their separate ways. By that time my sister and I remained in the house while my mom still supported us, but we eventually had to put our sons in daycare, and get our own job, which we did. We also took advantage of the programs for single moms at that time which included a daycare stipend, food stamps, and

WIC. We were now a part of the government system that was designed for temporary assistance. I'm thankful that the programs were there at the time, but we didn't have plans on remaining on the system, so we went to work.

I landed a position doing accounting work with the State of Florida, and they offered free tuition to its employees. I took advantage of the benefit and enrolled back in the local university. I stayed on my job for two years, prior to leaving and enrolling in the university full-time. After hard work and perseverance, I was able to finish my degree in two and a half years, taking twenty-one hours a semester, while remaining on honor roll, serving in leadership roles, and being a single mother to my son. It was a journey, and I'm thankful for the support of my family, and my son's godmother because I wouldn't have been able to achieve my goal.

I graduated and moved away for my first teaching position in South Florida because my mom was a newlywed and I wanted to be close by. I ended up getting married, and then divorced, and then married again, and divorced again to the same individual. I don't want to focus on that in this book but do understand that finances were not addressed in the marriage, and we had all the outward signs of success, yet without a real savings, no investments, and the only wise decision we made together was purchasing a home, which we almost lost.

Six years later, I ended up moving to a new state, remarrying, and by this time I had three boys. One from a previous relationship, and the other two children were conceived during from my previous marriage. My new husband and I were both educators, and were making a decent salary, in fact we made over six figures combined. Prior to us getting married, I lived in an apartment in a gated community with lots of amenities and conveniences yet found myself struggling a bit initially. My bills were paid, but I had more month than money. The cost of living was more than what I was accustomed to, and I had expenses of daycare and aftercare added to my non-existent budget because I didn't know anyone in Georgia, and I left my support system.

Eventually, I got it together and I began paying off my debts including my car, and credit card, so this helped tremendously. There was still no savings or investments in sight. When my husband and I decided that we were going to be together, I kept my apartment until we got married, and then we moved into his three-story home. We were doing well initially, both our vehicles were paid off, we refinanced the home to lower the payment, and we were eating out and shopping on a regular basis. We still didn't have any money saved, nor did we have any types of investments aside from our 401k's.

My husband came from a background where his mother worked at the local hospital prior to her retiring, but from her earnings she was able to buy a home, save, and take care of her family along with my husband's father. He grew up struggling financially when he was younger, living with his grandparents and cousins in one home, but his mother did adopt the principle of saving your money. Well, when you put both of our financial backgrounds together you can see that we were not where we needed to be financially. We fell into the living from paycheck to paycheck, borrowing from family members periodically, and struggling financially. We had everything that exhibited success, yet we were headed to a financial pit.

We eventually started waking up and devising a plan to financial freedom. The first thing we learned was to pay ourselves first. After paying our tithes, we began saving in pure gold through a company called Karat Bars. Then we started getting rid of everything that was suffocating us: the house, the car, etc. During all of this, I was offered a job abroad, and this couldn't have come at a more perfect time. We were already letting things go, and we were looking for a new start, and new direction. It wasn't until recently when we moved abroad when we began living again. We were away from all the pressures of life, and we left the pay-check-to-pay-check mentality, and began building generational wealth, saving, investing, and securing a future for our children, grandchildren, and future generations.

Today we are less than a year from being debt free (except for some student loans, but we're making payments and believing for total debt cancellation), and we have a savings, and we have money that we are investing, and making multiple streams of income. All of this took renewing our mind and scheduling our success. It's important to locate where you are for you to move forward. That's why it's important to include my journey to help pinpoint where all the wrong thinking, the poverty mindset, and the financial bondage originated. The struggle was real, but amid it all there is a way to win with a kingdom mindset.

CHAPTER 5: MONEY MATTERS - THE KINGDOM MINDSET

Somewhere down the road some people have been convinced that money doesn't matter, you don't need money, and it's evil. In fact, one of the most misquoted scriptures that I've heard for years is found in I Timothy 6:10: "For the love of money is the root of all evil: which while some coveted after; they have pierced themselves through with." If you think that something is evil, naturally you begin to repel it. That's why getting another job or trying to earn more money is not a solution to a spiritual problem. The problem is that when a person's mind has not been renewed to the purpose for money, they will always have a distorted view, and look at money with the wrong pair of lenses. The scripture in I Timothy 6:10 does say that the love of money is the root of all evil.

It's very apparent today when you see family betraying one another, marriages destroyed, crime, murder, political corruption, and all manner of evil. If we were to back test any of these transgressions, the root cause will always be money. I've seen people suffer for lack of money especially during natural disasters. Tornadoes, hurricanes, and different forces of nature have swept through communities most times leaving people with very little resources. Then people find themselves dependent on the government and federal funded programs to help rebuild. Thank God for this type of assistance, but sometimes the people still suffer if things aren't done in a timely manner.

I remember specifically when Hurricane Katrina swept through Louisiana, and several families where misplaced. I witnessed this because I received several students in my class who had been displaced from the hurricane. The families basically had to start from ground zero and begin rebuilding. I know even having money, and savings of some sort could have made a difference in the lives of many of the families. When money is not readily available, decisions can sometimes be made that you normally wouldn't have entertained. For instance, growing up I saw single moms remain in unhealthy relationships with men for the sake of having stability and the basics such as food, shelter, and clothing for themselves and their children. Then you have people who try to keep up with everyone with having nice homes, expensive cars, and fancy clothes, all in the name of debt. Outwardly they look as if they have it going on, but in actuality because of their lavish lifestyle, and lack of savings, they are drowning in debt. The debt collectors are calling constantly, they're having to hide their vehicle in fear of the repo man taking it away any minute, and their mortgage is heading toward foreclosure. This is the perfect example of when the bible speaks about the borrower been servant to the lender in Proverbs 22:7, "The rich ruleth over the poor, and the borrower is servant to the lender." It's a slave and master relationship, and it was never meant to be this way. We have been given the authority to tell our money what to do, and not have it as our master.

There are also people who go to church every Sunday, but they don't believe that Christians should have money. The problem is that they aren't operating from the kingdom mindset. From what I've seen in my own experience, these are the churches where most of the members suffer lack, and they're always having fish fries, and other fundraisers to help meet the budget. They try and justify this by saying things that Jesus was born in a lonely manger, and he had nowhere to lay his head. If you examine the scripture, you will find that Jesus was born a king, and the Magi brought him gold, frankincense, and myrrh. This doesn't sound like a broke Jesus.

Usually when I see people frown upon Christians who happen to be prospering financially, it's an indication that they lack understanding of the kingdom mindset, and they haven't released their faith in the fact that wills for them to prosper. Faith comes by hearing, and hearing by the word of God, so if you're not hearing about the kingdom and how it operates as it pertains to prospering, then you can't build faith in that area. Then it becomes much easier to point the finger at those that have laid hold of the kingdom truths. Even as a believer, it takes money to finance the kingdom of God. Not having enough money to pay your bills or help others in need is not the will of God. Especially when you read in the bible the promise that God made to Abraham, and since we are his descendants, it holds true for us today, "I will bless those who bless you, and whoever curses you I will curse; and all peoples on the earth will be blessed through you." (Genesis 12:3).

There is work that needs to be done in the body of Christ concerning money because money does matter, and the kingdom is within us. Everything that we need that pertains to life and godliness has already been put on the inside. It's just a matter of manifesting it in the natural and releasing your faith to receive it. There are a lot of people who spend their entire lifetime searching for riches, but the riches are already within us.

CHAPTER 6: MONEY WITH A PURPOSE

Money has a purpose and if we don't understand its purpose then it can cause major problems. I had to renew my mind even in my own understanding of the purpose of money. Up until recently, I participated in hyperinflation. Whenever I received a raise on my job I thought that meant go out and buy a new house, a new car, or create more debt. It never dawned on me that it was an opportunity to come out of debt, live below my means, and free of more money for the kingdom of God. There is no other way to put it: I was basically a fool who didn't know what to do with my money. The bible will tell you exactly who you are, and what you are so there's no need to get offended. The bible is as real as it comes. The beautiful part about the bible is that it will correct you, and then provide proper instructions. It just doesn't leave you in your mess.

I remember reading about the rich young ruler, and he accumulated all this wealth and he was asking Jesus what he could do to inherit eternal life. Jesus began naming the things that he should be doing to inherit eternal life. The rich young ruler was proud of himself because it appeared that he met all the requirements that Jesus named. The lesson that Jesus was trying to show him is that no matter how many things he's done, he still lacked one thing, and that we are all in need of a Savior. The rubber met the road when Jesus finally said to the rich young ruler in Matthew 19:21-22: "Jesus said to him, 'If you want to be perfect, go, sell what you have and give to the poor, and you will have treasure in heaven; and come follow Me.' But when the young man heard that saying, he went away sorrowful, for he had great possessions."

I used to read the bible and judge the people for the decisions that they made, especially Adam and Eve. I used to say, "They messed it up for everyone," until it dawned on me–I probably would have messed it up too. Even the situation with the rich young ruler is not far-fetched from us today. When the Holy Spirit prompts my heart to give, instead of giving instantly, I sometimes think about the bills I must pay, how much money I'm going to have left if I give, and what I could've purchased with the money. The tithing part is not the issue…

it's the giving from the ninety percent because somewhere down the line I selectively forget that all of it belongs to him.

The other example is given as a parable in Luke 12 when the rich man ran out of room to store his abundance, and he decided to tear down his barns and build bigger ones to store his crops. God came back with a rebuttal for him, and it went something like this: "But God said to him, 'Fool! This night your soul will be required of you; then whose will those things be which you have provided?'"

It's same thing I mentioned before about what happened when I'd get a raise. God is such a great teacher because he used parables to show us ourselves because sometime pride won't allow us to see that that's how we are at times. I know that I used to ask the questions like, "What's the purpose of having money if it's not meant to enjoy? What should I be doing with my money? The first thing that we must understand is that money is here for us to enjoy, and we were meant to have money, but money was not meant to have us. God in his infinite wisdom knew that money could also be destroyer in the hands of wrong people. They're using their money to create mass weapons of destruction, buy drugs, and finance hate groups, while they're financing mission trips, building orphanages, and doing the work of the ministry. Money in of itself it's not bad; it's a matter of whose hands it's in.

I later discovered that money is also an amplifier to a man's character. Have you ever heard people say things like, "When I become a millionaire, I going to tithe," or "When I get some money, I'm going go to help the poor." Whatever we're doing with our money right now is a pretty good indication of what we will do when we get more money. The money itself is not going to help us make better decisions, in fact it's just going to provide you with more choices. For instance, if a person is cheating on their spouse and going to hotels to meet up, having more money will give them an opportunity to continue to cheat in Vegas or in another country. Having the money did not change the behavior but it allowed for sin to be committed on a greater scale.

I love how it works on the flip side too. If you have a heart for missions and you're already giving, having more money will provide you an opportunity to visit the countries you're supporting, give more money, or help with missions on a larger scale. The first scripture that I read and gained an understanding of not only when it came to money but with everything, was Matthew 6:33: "But seek ye first the kingdom of God and his righteousness, and all these things shall be added unto you." This scripture lets me know that kingdom business comes first, and all these other things that I think I want, shall be added. The paradigm shift came for me when I realized that money should be exchanged for souls. This is the exact revelation that could shut down the kingdom of darkness. If we view money as an opportunity to snatch a soul from going to eternal damnation, that within itself is powerful.

We talked about what God considers a fool with money but watch who he calls wise. Proverbs 11:30: "The fruit of the righteous is a tree of life; and he that winneth souls is wise." The questions that we might ponder are already contained in the word of God. "God how do I become wise?" God answers, "Win Souls."

The other answer for what do we do with money came by way of when God was speaking to Abraham. "And I will make you into a great nation, I will bless you, I will make your name great, and you will be a blessing." (Genesis 12:2). This scripture not only talks about when we are blessed with money, but it's a reminder that the only reason that we are blessed, is so that we can be a blessing to others. Money has a purpose, and it's not just for our own selfish gain.

7 KEYS TO P.O.P. (PROSPER ON PURPOSE)

Chapter 7: Key #1 See God as Your Only Source 27
Chapter 8: Key #2 Renew Your Mind 32
Chapter 9: Key #3 See Your Job as Your Seed 36
Chapter 10: Key #4 Begin Speaking Life 40
Chapter 11: Key #5 Increase Your Financial I.Q. 44
Chapter 12: Key #6 Teach Your Children the Language of Wealth 49
Chapter 13: Key #7 Begin Empowering Others 55
About the Author 60

CHAPTER 7: KEY #1 SEE GOD AS YOUR ONLY SOURCE

The first key to P.O.P. (Prosper on Purpose) is, you must see God as not just a source, but as your ONLY source. It took me a while to understand that because I was depended on everything but God as my source. It's easy to consider everything else but God as your source. The reason how I know this is that the average person sees their job as their source. I've been there where I thought that if I didn't have a job, my needs would not be met. The first time God showed me differently is when I left my first marriage, and I left my job with only a two-day notice. I hadn't saved much money at the time, in fact I barely had enough money to stay in a hotel for two days to handle business, put gas in my truck to head to my Mom's house, and provide food for my children and me for a couple of days. I didn't consider what life was going to be without a husband, without a job, and without a true savings, I just knew that my kids and I were suffering, and I wanted out. At this point it had become dangerous to remain in the marriage because the spirit of addiction had taken over completely. I left with very few of my items; I basically packed one set of clothes for each of us, and grabbed a couple of important papers, leaving everything else behind.

Once I arrived at my Mom's house after a couple of weeks, I found myself applying for food stamps to help with food. I was given more than enough food stamps, so much that I would gather food, and take it to a well-known place in my hometown where the homeless people hung out. I didn't just deliver the food, but I befriended some of the people I met there. I would spend hours sitting around talking to them as my then toddler fed the ducks at the lake. I knew that I was in a broken state at the time, and I couldn't teach until I became emotionally stable.

I stayed with my mom for three months, and by that time God had provided a job, secured us a place to live, and provided everything new to move into our apartment. The job came by divine appointment because I was home one day at my mom's apartment watching television, and the phone rang. I decided to answer the phone, and when I picked up, the person on the other line was looking for a person who apparently applied for a substitute teaching position. I eagerly replied, "You have the wrong number, but I'm a certified teacher who moved here recently." I was asked to come to the school the very next day, and I was hired immediately. The principal knew my entire family, and not only that, she was confident that I could do the job. I later filled out the application, and I ended spending three years there until I heard God call me to move to Atlanta, Georgia. God was showing me that he was my source, and that he knew how to prosper me everywhere I go. The conclusion of the matter is that prosperity isn't about money, it's about wholeness. If we only think about prosperity as money, we are missing out on the fullness that God has for us. He wants to be the source of everything. Even the things that we think that we can do well in our own strength, God is saying that he wants it all.

There are so many other testimonies that I have that clearly show the hand of God, but I share one that happened to me recently. I went home to visit family and when I went for my annual physical, my doctor discovered that my fibroids had grown significantly, and they needed medical attention immediately. I scheduled the surgery with my doctor, and I was hoping to recover stateside since my job was abroad. In order to secure my job, I had to go back abroad to my job because by this time, it was already two weeks into the new school year. I returned to my position, but since I was on medical leave in the United States, it wasn't approved abroad, which ultimately docked me three months without pay until the proper procedures were followed. During this season I was separated from my husband and children because we enrolled them in school thinking that we would be there a while until after I recovered.

At this point not only is my family and I separated from one another, but I was without a salary for three whole months. To be honest, I would have been concerned, and trying to figure things out, but I can clearly remember God saying, "I'm your only source, I'll supply all of your needs according to your riches and glory through Christ Jesus." This is exactly what happened, Jehovah Jireh showed himself strong in my situation. I had people giving to me from my job, at church, and neighbors, and it wasn't because I was asking.

I remember one day I came home and my lights were off. I walked over to the electric company and explained my situation, and I asked them to turn the lights back on because I didn't have any income at the time. The gentleman that was helping me explained to me that there wasn't anything he could do, but his supervisor was passing by and overheard the conversation and told him to turn my lights back on.

The phone company started this point system for every time you pay your phone bill, you earned credits. My friend and I took advantage of the buy one get one free offers, and spent several days at Applebee's, TGIF's, and a couple of other restaurants who participated in the reward system. The help that we need may not come traditionally, or as we think it should, but once we take God out of the box and allow him to move, he will go to work on our behalf.

I must also share this with parents who have children that are leaving for college and they may not have a scholarship, but God can work in unconventional ways. My oldest son finished high school at the local private school that leads into the university. When he graduated from high school, he didn't have a scholarship; although he could've accepted a track scholarship from somewhere in Kentucky. Although his dad and I didn't marry, he was beyond supportive to the point that he lived with him during high school. I remember thinking about having to pay my part for his college education because I didn't save anything toward it, just because of lack of preparation and not thinking, to be honest. I think I paid for one semester throughout his entire time in college, and he received a stipend for most of the time for filming and editing for the college's football team. The stipend covered his classes and afforded him free meals and some of the privileges of the athletes. It was almost as if he had a full ride scholarship minus the housing, but his dad had already blessed him with a home by his sophomore year. "God will do exceedingly and abundantly above all that we ask or think, according to the power that works in us." (Ephesians 3:20).

The last thing I want to address is that when you know that God is your source, you don't have to walk in fear when it comes to a job. I have experienced it and I see it happens all the time when you have supervisors and superiors who treat you unkind for whatever reason. They make it appears they can fire you at any time for whatever reason. When you have prayed for a job, and God grants you that position, that means that he put you there, and he's the only one that can remove you. "For promotion cometh neither from the east, nor from the west, nor from the south. But God is the judge; he putteth down one, and setteth up another." (Psalm 76:6-7).

If we're not careful we can end up walking in fear for not knowing or understanding what the word of God is saying. When we believe and understand that God is our source, we can work unto him, and know that if a door closes, he already has one waiting for us. Understanding God is our only source brings about great peace and freedom.

Notes/Reflection

CHAPTER 8: KEY #2 RENEW YOUR MIND

The second key to P.O.P. (Prosper on Purpose) is to renew your mind when it comes to prosperity. When the idea first came to write this book, I thought that I would focus on building generational wealth and share my testimony and journey about how God dealt with me when it came to my finances. Little did I know that the book would take a turn and cause me to reveal more about my own journey, and how this can help others, and how I overcame the spirit of mammon that's robbing people of reaching their kingdom fringe benefits. (God daily loads us up with benefits.)

This book is not just about money because we will miss what God is trying to do entirely. Renewing my mind about prosperity helped me to stop chasing money. I even concluded that if I never reach millionaire status, its's all good because the quality of the life that I live and finishing well are important. I have seen a lot of people lately lacking in health, relationships, and the fruit of the spirit, but if I'm having to spend it on medical bills, counseling sessions, etc., that is a sign that wholeness is missing from my life.

Although Jesus died and gave us everything that we need that pertains to life and godliness, if we don't know what benefits were included, although it has been made available to us, we will not be able to take advantage of it. A very practical example is when I purchased my cars. To be honest, I rarely read the manual prior to buying the car, I generally depend on the salesman to show me everything. The last vehicle I purchased, the car could park itself, but I forgot how to activate it, so I had to refer to the manual.

Joyce Meyer says, "Enjoy where you are on the way to where you are going." That is a life changing statement for me because some people plan to enjoy their life after retirement. As a matter of fact, God speaks of being able to enjoy the fruit of your labor, so that's a blessing within itself. It is vitally important that we don't use the world's definition of success, which boils down to a nice house, a nice car, a good job, and money in the bank. I've read so many inspiring stories where people worked as janitors, cafeteria workers, and other jobs that have been classified as "blue collar" jobs. These people managed to put food on the table, buy a home, and put their children through college. This really made me think; how is this possible? The first thing I discovered was that it was God's grace and mercy on the lives of people. Grace is God's unmerited favor when we get what we don't deserve, and mercy is when we deserve something, but we didn't get it just like what Jesus did for us on the cross. We were all guilty before God, and punishment was warranted, but thank you God that the penalty for sin was accepted through his son Jesus.

I've come to realize that someone who makes $30,000 can live better than someone who makes $100,000 because at the end of the day, it's not about how much money you make, it's about how much you have left once you pay all your bills.

All these thoughts lead to a question: What does renewing your mind entail? It requires changing our thoughts for God's thoughts. I had to adopt a new mindset about money. I had to move myself out of the way and think in terms of being a steward instead of an owner. This meant that I was managing God's money, not doing what I wanted to do with the money. Moving from owner to steward takes the help of the Holy Spirit because the natural man is going to want to fight against the Spirit. The flesh will rise up and convince you that you worked for that money, so you can do what you want to do with it.

Renewing the mind is also important because the spirit of mammon makes you believe that if you give, you are losing instead of gaining. This type of mindset prevents you from receiving because not only is giving a principle, but it's a law. That means that it will work for anyone who gets involved in the process.

Have you ever heard the saying, "You will reap what you sow?" Not only is it a saying, but it is a biblical principle. A lot of times the saying is quoted when someone has been done wrong and they use it to let the offender know that they will reap whatever they have sown toward the other person. The scripture points out in Galatians 6:7, "Do not be deceived, God is not mocked; for whatever a man sows, that he will also reap." This scripture was a reminder to do good, and not to grow weary in doing so. Jesus left the greatest examples of sowing by using parables. He was so brilliant that he always used others as an example to show people themselves, and to teach them a lesson.

Renewing your mind is crucial because money is simply an amplifier of who you are. If you are a giver, you will give more, if you are an alcoholic, you will remain an alcoholic, but you'll buy finer liquor. This isn't based on what I think, it's based on what I know from experience. We must pray and ask God for wisdom, and we must desire to do whatever God asks us to do with his money. After all, we must desire God more than anything on this earth, and here's a secret that I discovered that will carry us from earth to glory: when we get God, we get everything!

Notes/Reflection

CHAPTER 9: KEY #3 SEE YOUR JOB AS YOUR SEED

The third key to P.O.P. (Prosper on Purpose) is to begin to see your job as your seed. I have worked a couple of other jobs prior to my teaching career, but they were short term assignments. During some of the assignments I found myself mumbling and complaining, not realizing that even those jobs that I didn't seem to value, still had a role to play in reaching my destiny. My very first job was at Dairy Queen when I was fifteen years old and still in high school. I was excited about this job, because all my other friends had jobs at the major fast food restaurants like McDonald's, Burger King, and Wendy's, etc. I didn't realize it at the time, but that job was teaching me balance, how to manage my money, and how to be accountable.

    I remember my manager moving me from making the orders to multi-tasking and making the orders and ringing up the customers. There were other workers there who were older at the time, but she saw something in me I didn't see in myself at the time. I stayed there for over a year until they were robbed, and the owner was shot in front of me. That experience was devastating, but I was thankful to be alive and I realized that I will always be grateful for having the chance to work at Dairy Queen as my first job. It reminds me of the scripture that says don't despise humble beginnings.

    While in high school, I had the wonderful opportunity to gain skills through a class called CBE. This class prepared you with job skills to work in a professional setting. I was able to secure a job at a major bank as a coder, and this job lasted up until I went to college. This was my first encounter of learning how to work with people with varying personalities. They were much older than me, and sometimes they weren't always professional. This job was preparing me for life because I have encountered situations on my job that weren't always favorable, but I was blessed to be able to handle them in a professional manner, without losing my cool. I didn't know anything about the fruits of the spirit, but I know God was extending his grace to me even back then. I'm sharing these experiences because I know what it's like to work a job and have a passion for something else. During these seasons we must view our job as our seed.

IT'S TIME TO P.O.P. PROSPER ON PURPOSE

I moved prematurely once because I didn't quite understand my job as my seed. I really have a passion for writing books, plays, songs, etc., basically any type of writing. I remember at one time I had to quit my job to care for my grandmother until she received the medical attention and provisions that she needed. I really wanted to write full-time too, but it wasn't quite time for me to leave my job and pursue writing full time. I didn't realize that my job could finance my dream. We can have a dream and God will make provision for our dream, but we shouldn't quit or job immediately unless we have really heard from God. When people start viewing their job as a burden, and don't see it as a blessing and a means to drive them to their dream, they may end up quitting prematurely.

I found the best thing you can do while working your current job is to see yourself working your dream right where you are. This changed my life forever because when I went to work, I did my job with joy and to the glory of God. I realized that I wasn't stuck, and one day I'd be operating in my passion, but it was important to be faithful just where I was. I became kinder to my co-workers, I was able to submit to my superiors, and I stopped all the mumbling and complaining. Then I asked myself the paramount question: if I were the employer would I hire me?

When we are faithful over another man's dream or vision, we are setting ourselves up for others to pour into our vision when it's time. Seeing your job as a seed brings about a blessing of honor and favor. Allow your job to drive you to your dream.

Recently my company terminated a lot of people for various reasons. Usually when you see terminations, it's attributed to poor performance. In this instant, this was not the case for everyone. Some people had been with the company for over five years, which was considered a long time. I gathered three things from this since it came so close to home, and it could have happened to any of us: 1) remember God as your only source; 2) make sure you have multiple streams of income; and 3) make sure you have at least three months of income saved. It was confirmation that having a linear income is just not enough.

Downsizing is becoming more prevalent no matter where you live or work, and although technology is a wonderful tool, jobs are being replaced by innovation of technology. When we think about a natural seed that is planted in the ground, eventually it will yield a harvest of whatever is planted. In order to Prosper on Purpose, we must be intentional about planting good seeds for the companies that employ us, especially if we are moving toward entrepreneurship. There isn't anything that we plant in the kingdom that won't reap a harvest.

Notes/Reflection

CHAPTER 10: KEY #4 BEGIN SPEAKING LIFE

The fourth key to P.O.P. (Prosper on Purpose) is to begin speaking life. In the book of Ezekiel, it asks the question, "Can these dry bones live?" I was at a point in my life that I was asking, "Can these drowning finances live?" The answer to both questions was an emphatic, "YES!" The same is true for you as well if you're in the same predicament. When I realized that I had to begin speaking life into my finances, I had to begin decreeing things. That's what happens in the kingdom, God has given us the ability to decree a thing and it shall be so. The entire earth was created by God speaking, and that's how everything was made. Once we become born again we become speaking spirits. I begin to see why God said in his word that life and death are in the power of our tongue. We have that same power to create heaven on earth today. That's why words are one of the most important power-producing gifts that we possess.

Half of the financial problems that I was experiencing was not only coming from a poverty mindset, but it also came from what I was speaking regarding my finances. It was impossible for me to experience victory in my finances when I was constantly speaking negatively against my finances. You can have what you say or say what you have. I heard this from a preacher a long time ago, but it didn't register for a while. I was speaking and saying exactly what I saw. "If it's not one thing, it's another." "We're never going to be able to come out of debt." "Every time I turn around, there's something." "Money don't grow on trees."

All these statements negate or go against the word of God. It's one thing to hear the word or God, but until it became a rhema word, and I received a revelation of this truth, I couldn't operate in it. This became the turning point because I stopped declaring what I was seeing. This was the very essence of faith. Faith is the substance of things hoped for and the evidence of things not yet seen. I began reading the word and standing on the promises. Even when things happened that negatively affected our finances, I would not use my mouth to speak against what was happening.

Recently, we faced a situation that required a great portion of my salary. I looked at the situation and I began to thank God. This wasn't because I welcomed the situation, it was because God gave us the ability to handle the financial situation. We did not miss a beat, and it didn't alter our standard of living. In fact, we were able to invest and save more. This is the kind of thing that doesn't make sense in the natural. We begin operating in Kingdom principles because we made Jesus the Lord of our finances. Our finances are no longer our business once we make Jesus the Lord over our finances and receive him as our only source.

Scripture declares that life and death are in the power of the tongue. I remember reading about a famous comedian who has since past away, and during an interview he stated that he wouldn't live past a certain age, believe it or not, he died at that very age. I don't think we realize how important our words are and how they produce. In order to protect our words, it's important that we guard our eye gate and our ear gate because these are the two areas that plant things in our heart. Out of the abundance of the heart, the mouth speaketh so whatever we have been filling our hearts with, that's exactly what comes out.

Recently there have been many issues where leaders and business owners have made racists comments. When these things happen, I automatically know that it's a matter of a heart. It doesn't matter how much we long for a public apology, until that person's heart is changed, there really won't be true repentance.

It doesn't matter what appears to be dead in our lives, whether it be relationships, finances, or health and wellness, we must begin speaking life into it – which is ultimately the word of God. When your bank account says depleted, you must declare, "I'll never be broke another day in my life." According to Philippians 4:19, "And my God shall supply all my needs according to His riches and glory in by Christ Jesus."

Identify a challenge you may be experiencing now, search the scripture that provides a solution to your problem, and then begin speaking that scripture. My finances were sick and needed healing, so I began to apply every scripture that related to me prospering. We must believe that it is the will of God to prosper us and then began speaking it. If you struggle with believing that God wants you to prosper, begin praying, "God help my unbelief," and then fill your eyes and ears with the word pertaining to your prosperity. I also recommend that you begin writing down exactly what you want to see in your finances and begin making confessions toward what you're believing God for.

My first faith confession was, "I'm out of debt, my needs are met, I have plenty more to lay in store." I begin to slowly see my debt disappear. Today I'm not drowning in debt, and I'm tackling my student loan debt which I thought for sure was the boogie man. I'm no longer afraid to face where I am financially, and deal with it. In order to Prosper on Purpose, begin speaking life once you identify where you are, write it down with the date, find scriptures to stand on, and begin make confessions.

Notes/Reflection

CHAPTER 11: KEY #5 INCREASE YOUR FINANCIAL I.Q.

The fifth key to P.O.P. (Prosper on Purpose), is to increase your Financial I.Q. I heard of I.Q. as it relates to academics, but it wasn't until recently that I discovered the word Financial I.Q. In my own definition, I would describe Financial I.Q. as your knowledge about money and how it works, and the ability to apply that knowledge.

I learned about balancing a checkbook in high school through a business course that provided me with job skills, and then actually found a job that could possibly lead into a career. I landed a job at the Capital City Bank in Tallahassee, and I stayed there until I began college. While working at the bank, I learned a couple of banking terms, but I wasn't out front as a teller. I worked upstairs coding and balancing checks using a machine. I came up in an era where everyone wrote checks. I even witnessed people writing bad checks, and I saw the horrendous bank fees attached to it, and the legal ramifications that came along with writing bad checks. By the time I entered my freshman year of college, I fell prey to credit card debt. I started living a lavish lifestyle on credit and renting cars for my weekend get-a-ways. Saving was nowhere on my agenda. Even when I got a raise, in my head I would have already spent it before it even arrived. The only terms I understood was credits and debits, and I had more credits than debits.

To be honest, it wasn't until the last couple years of my adult life that I begin increasing my Financial I.Q. I looked to Mentors who were already where I wanted to be. It wasn't enough for me to read books, but I wanted living testaments of people who found financial freedom. I found those initial mentors in Mr. Michael Dalcoe and Mr. Ty Best, who are the top leaders of our Wealthbuilders World Wide Gold Saving Family. Joining a network marketing business was one of the first things I did to increase my Financial I.Q. This totally revolutionized my life because it caused me to read more books on finances, practice wealth principles, and learn how to talk less and listen more.

IT'S TIME TO P.O.P. PROSPER ON PURPOSE

As I said in the earlier chapter, I had the tithing part down, but I wasn't accustomed to doing things like paying myself first. The excellent leadership in the network marketing business I joined not only helped me increase my Financial I.Q., but helped me understand that gold was real money, and that I could build generational wealth for not only my children, but my children's children. The only gold I knew about was the gold that people wore on their body, or the gold that people had on their teeth. I didn't have a clue the pure gold came from a refinery, and it's actual rectangular shaped. I never fathomed that the dollar was depreciating, and no matter how many jobs we work, we can't outrun inflation. Gold still holds its value as it did years ago.

This company gave me the history of how President Nixon stopped money from being backed by gold; thereby causing inflation and the printing of money in thin air which depreciates its value. I never even fathomed owning gold before moving into this space of network marketing. Now I have the wonderful privilege of introducing people to the possibility of not only saving in gold, but literally owning their own business. I've been blessed to have close to 2,000 people on my team, and I'm still helping families find financial freedom through saving in gold. That's the power of network marketing.

As you begin to help others, your business begins to grow. So here I was being introduced to words like fiat currency, gold bullion, and reading books by Robert Kiyosaki. I entered a whole new world that I never knew existed.

Then I watched this phenomenal woman for years come to events at our church at World Changers. I'd watched her T.V. shows Thicker Than Water and the Jewel Tankard Show. I always admired her from a distance because I could relate to her although she and her husband Ben Tankard were already multi-millionaires. She's very transparent, and I had experienced some of the things she shared in her personal testimony. I had written in my journal that I wanted to meet her personally, and I wanted to host a conference where she would be the speaker. I moved halfway across the world, and not only did I have an opportunity to meet with her, and talk with her one on one, but she also introduced me to the Forex market, and I joined her Millionaire's Club. I never fathomed that I could own gold, and it blew my mind that she introduced me to a debt free business that earns 5.3 trillion dollars a day in the foreign exchange market. I partnered up with her in a company that provides the educational platform to trade on Wall Street.

The new channels that dealt with money that I used to casually click past, now became my favorite channels. I used to change the channel on the T.V. when Dow Jones, or other Financial News would appear. All of a sudden, that changed once my mind was renewed towards money. I began looking at the market and reading charts to find out if it was a bullish or bearish market. I learned all the currency pairs and begin trading regularly. The trading became so much fun that I had to narrow my schedule down to specific days and times that I traded so that I could maintain balance.

Jewel is now one of my Financial Mentors, and not only did she introduce me to trading foreign currency, she stretched me in other areas of my life that were mediocre. Her Millionaires Club is creating millionaires, and one reason for her success is that she's warm, caring, and she really wants everyone to win. She's a savvy business woman, which I love, because she has several successful businesses on top of her success as a top earner in our company. She balances her family life and businesses, which is important to me. I believe in multiple streams of income, and some people may frown at the fact that I'm involved in two companies, but as Jewel Tankard says, "You Can Have It All."

The most important thing you can do aside from reading books on finances, starting a network marketing business, and getting a Financial Mentor, is to go back to the Creator of all things, God. The word of God is ultimately the road map to success and the best way to increase our Financial I.Q. God uses the Holy Spirit to lead and guide us, and since we live in this natural realm, he has put people on the earth to lead and guide us as well. It's important that we understand this along our personal journey.

It was through prayer that all these opportunities and people came into my life. I call them divine appointments. I couldn't have received these things in my life any sooner because I wasn't prepared to receive them. This is important because once you pray for wisdom and understanding, and you really want to experience change in your finances, just simply ask God, and he will put you in the right places, with the right people, and at the right time. If I would have limited God, I never would have met Michael Dalcoe, Ty Best, or Jewel Tankard. Although I had seen Jewel Tankard on several occasions, it wasn't until I moved to another country that we established a relationship. It would have been logical for me to meet her in the United States, but that wasn't God's Plan. When we sit back and let God be God, he does an amazing job!

In order to Prosper on Purpose, we must increase our Financial I.Q. by surrounding ourselves with Financial Mentors, reading books on Finances, and most importantly, seeking God, asking him for wisdom as it relates to our finances. This also may mean changing your circle. I know that I was resistant in the beginning, but it was because I didn't understand. I can no longer allow people to influence me when it comes to money who aren't experiencing success. Be prepared for people to walk away from you because you will desire to be with people you can connect with on a higher level. It's not to say that you have to dismiss people from your life, it's just that they will eventually come along with you for the journey, or leave. You have to be okay with God prospering you, and not feel guilty. It is the will of God to prosper us, but everyone won't receive the promise.

Notes/Reflection

CHAPTER 12: KEY #6 TEACH YOUR CHILDREN THE LANGUAGE OF WEALTH

The sixth key to P.O.P. (Prosper on Purpose) is to teach your children the language of wealth. Growing up I didn't know anything about finances. The only thing I understood is that people went to work, on Friday they cashed their check, paid their bills, and then they looked forward to doing the same thing the following week. I don't recall planning for family vacations, or sitting around the table discussing money at all, that was what they called, "grown folks," business, and children were not allowed to partake in these type conversations. The only thing I recall is my Mom usually working two jobs to help make ends meet.

My mom was a hard worker, and she did whatever it took to make sure that my sister and I had our basic needs met. She always had respectable jobs during the day because she was very intelligent, and she had an amazing work ethic that her superiors always respected. I do remember that my mom was working an Administrative Assistant position with the State of Florida by day, and she was a waitress at night. This was only for a short period of time, but I loved when she came home and allowed us to count the tips, and she would usually give us the change.

When I graduated from high school, I witnessed my mom working for one of the State Representatives in Florida and starting a business with a partner by opening a Nail Shop in our hometown of Tallahassee, Florida. The business really began to flourish, and college students and local workers came to the shop to get their nails done, with their unique designs. Doing nails was a hidden talent that my mom didn't even know that she had, she simply had a desire. I admire my mom for that because she took her desire further by going to Nail School and she worked from her home until she was able to open her own salon. One of the best things about the whole thing that brings about great memories is that my maternal grandmother (Hazel), retired from the Florida State Mental Hospital, and she helped my mom in the Nail Shop by greeting customers and scheduling nail appointments. Grandma looked after the shop while Mom worked her full-time job with the State Representative, Al Lawson. She willingly washed the white towels daily, and she would bring them back to the shop crisp, and neatly folded.

Whenever time permitted, grandma would allow Mom to paint her nails and toes with designs, while my Uncle Anton would keep her hair freshly done with the latest styles. Having my family work in the beauty industry was a blessing to me especially when I started college. Fashionable nails and hair was a must at Florida A & M University, so having people in my family who specialized in these two areas saved me tons of money, and I didn't realize it until I was much older. God was blessing my family even back then. It finally dawned me that although I wasn't engaged in a conversation about money and entrepreneurship, I was shown the way through my grandfather and my mother through their successful businesses.

My mom eventually closed the Nail Shop because something went wrong with the partnership, and my grandmother passed away. This was a very sad time because I saw something go away from my mom when these two major events occurred in her life. My mom eventually started doing nails in her home again, but that came to halt when she re-married and her new husband couldn't endure the chemicals. This showed me something very important about relationships because when God gives us a gift, we must guard it and not let anything separate us from our passion, not even a relationship.

Although I witnessed more showing than telling, it was important for me to teach my children the language of wealth. Although the school system does a great job in preparing students for some things in life, financial literacy is an area that's rarely discussed. In fact, the only course that I had that came remotely to teaching me about finances was a class I had to take in high school that was a Basic Accounting course to meet the Math requirements for graduation. I could not depend on the school system to educate my children about money. My son who's already graduated from college really didn't benefit when my Financial I.Q. increase because I didn't quite have everything together when he was younger. The only thing he witnessed was when I purchased our first home before he started kindergarten. His dad filled in the gaps in that area and taught him all the ropes.

My son's dad came from a family who were educated, and they were also entrepreneurs. Although his father and I never married, he did a wonderful job in preparing him for the real world. By the time he was a sophomore in college, my son was already a homeowner, he had a debt free car, and he finished his degree at Florida Agricultural & Mechanical University without owing Sallie Mae, or any of the other lending institutions. The curse has been broken as far as accumulating debt and struggling financially.

My last two children witnessed a bit of struggle but they may have been a bit confused because on the outside it looked as though we were winning. We moved from an apartment to a three-story home, and we went from one vehicle to four vehicles. There was a point when they even attended a private military school. This happened when I left the single life and married my current husband. The problem was that we were living above our means, and accumulating debt. We were basically living from paycheck to paycheck, and robbing Peter to pay Paul. This went on for a couple of years until we finally realized that insanity was doing the same thing, expecting different results. I was determined that my children would not repeat this pattern. The first thing they learned is that debt is not good. It's so funny right now because they used to chant, "No More Debt." They learned this from a preacher who would say this often.

When I read Robert Kiyosaki's book, Rich Dad Poor Dad, I was shocked to learn that a house is not an asset, but considered a debt. I knew we had to do something about this issue of debt. We've finally managed to overcome the prison of debt apart from our student loans, and one credit card for renting cars and other things requiring a credit card. The good news is that we no longer use credit cards to live, and we pay them to avoid enormous finance charges.

In the process of moving toward debt freedom, we've also managed to rebuild our credit. The different mindset for us now is if we can't buy it with cash, we really don't need it. We're even thinking on this level when it comes to houses and cars. We can put kingdom principles into practice to obtain even our material possessions.

It's important for children to understand at a young age that they don't have to be in the entertainment business or settle to be prosperous. The images on music videos and T.V. usually sell them a false dream, but the reality is that it's possible to live a good life by investing and teaching children how to let money work for them, instead of them having to work for it.

This book is about the beginning of moving into Prospering on Purpose, the next book will deal with showing and telling when the manifestations show up. My children understand the principles of tithing, paying yourself first, and investing. These are the principles that I missed in my childhood. They understand words that I didn't learn and understand until I was an adult. Words like money quadrant, foreign exchange market, inflation, bearish market, bullish market, and many others. The most important revelation that has been imparted to them is that God is their source, and they must seek ye first the kingdom of God and his righteousness, and all these things shall be added unto you. They also understand that it's the will of God to prosper them in every area of their lives. They can also recognize when someone is operating in the spirit of poverty.

We were watching a T.V. show that Chris Rock created in the early 90's called "Everybody Hates Chris." This was an example of the epitome of a family operating in complete poverty. The funny was hilarious, but everything they did was based on fear and the lack of money. They always focused on the lack of money and counted every penny. The children in the show knew that when it came to money, they better not ask their parents for anything. The dad in the show measured how much electricity cost, how much the food cost, and they always reminded them that they were in lack. The children had become conditioned to the spirit of poverty and they spoke the language of poverty. They never envisioned leaving their current situation, they had bought the lie of poverty.

I believe that you can learn from many things to help avoid pitfalls in life. The other part of the show that was brutally honest was when he dealt with racism, and how some people view African Americans by using stereotypes. We can't depend on anyone to teach our children the language of wealth, in fact it's our responsibility as parents. The government may fail people, some of the churches may not teach on it, we may have leaders who may be selfish with their own agenda, but one thing my children will tell anyone, the most important economy is the one in our own home.

In order to Prosper on Purpose, it's imperative to teach our children the language of by sowing the right seeds into their life. My youngest son has really grasped the language of wealth, and he repels poverty in all shapes and forms. He understands that school is important; however, he understands that it's not the end all and it's important to establish relationships. He knows that his network equals his net worth. This was also a paradigm shift for me because as an Educator, I remember that I was feeling that I failed as a parent if all my kids didn't go to college. Today I tell my kids to find your passion, get paid to do it effortlessly, and find a way to make money while you're sleeping.

Notes/Reflection

CHAPTER 13: KEY #7 BEGIN EMPOWERING OTHERS

The seventh key to P.O.P. (Prosper on Purpose) is to begin empowering others. The gifts and knowledge God imparts to us is never just for ourselves and our families – it's meant to be passed on to others. The bible says that people perish for a lack of knowledge, and this is true, we were perishing. The lack of understanding isn't just about lacking money, it's about how you can suffer in your health, marriage, and other areas.

I've witnessed people dying from the pressure of stress, and sometimes it was traced back to the lack of money. I've also witnessed marriages fail even in the church due to financial problems. My marriage has been strained due to lack of finances, and believe it or not, it can trickle down into your sex life. It's hard to be intimate when you have the cares of the world on your shoulder, and you're not operating in kingdom principles. That's why I felt it was important to begin sharing the knowledge I have gained with others. It wasn't just a matter of helping people to renew their mind in finances, and to P.O.P.-Prosper on Purpose, it was about helping people to improve their health, have healthy marriages, and live a life of heaven on earth, as God intended from the beginning in the Garden of Eden.

I love the song by Donald Lawrence that says, "Let's Get Back to Eden, and live on top of the world." I understood exactly what he was saying. It was God's purpose for us to have authority over everything on the earth. When Adam failed, God didn't fail, in fact, he put a plan to bring us back in the position of authority and establish his kingdom on the earth. Therefore, Jesus came to earth as the mediator to place things back in order so that God could have the authority again to bless his people. A penalty had to be paid for what Adam did, and Jesus was that perfect sacrifice. Salvation has been made available to all mankind. Salvation wasn't just a ticket to heaven, so we wouldn't go to hell, but it was a plan for God to reconcile mankind back to himself so that he could bless them. The bible is about a king and his kingdom. Religion has made people working too hard to achieve what God has already had Jesus finish. People begin operating in works instead of rest that's promised in

Hebrews 4. God wasn't resting because he was tired, he was resting because he was finished. The only requirement for us is to receive the rest that was offered unto us, is to receive it. This revelation must be understood to fully operate in any of the principles I've mentioned thus far in the book. Accepting Jesus Christ as our Lord and Savior is first base, and then we commit everything over to him including our finances, and this is what makes him not only our Savior, but our Lord. This is the first message that we must impart into others to empower them.

If you look around us, people who haven't accepted Jesus as Savior and Lord appear to prosper. They are winning when it comes to the material side, but recently I see more multi-millionaires taking their lives, compromising their values in the entertainment industry, and neglecting their family. My mentor Jewel Tankard always says "You Can Have It All." I love this because we can have it all, just without all the toil. The bible says that the blessing of the Lord, it maketh us rich, and addeth no sorrow to it.

There are several things that can be done to empower others, which include starting small groups in communities and teach the basics about finances. I started a Financial Empowerment Group while living abroad, and it took a while for the group to take form. After meeting two months and forming a leadership team, we finally came up with the vision to equip, educate, and empower others. We discussed exactly what that would look like, and we finally decided that before people can be equipped, educated, and empowered, we had to start with the basics by using simple principles. We designed a session called Finances 101 which deals with creating a vision board. This is the first and most powerful step because it's important to write the vision, make it plain as it states in Habakkuk. This gives a direction and allows people to create an action plan to go along with the vision board. This helps people to become intentional about what they wish to achieve in every area of their lives.

The next phase is to move toward locating where everyone is financially and creating a plan to become debt free. Finances 101 is also designed to help people create budgets while providing them with accountability partners. Then there are opportunities presented to create passive multiple streams of income. Remember the chapter where it talked about your job being your seed? The job is a linear income which basically allows you one way to make money. Once you pay your tithes and pay yourself first, then the money earned from the job can be put to work to create the passive multiple streams of income. I chose to show people how to save in gold through a company called Karat Bars, while creating passive income. This also supports saving and building generational wealth which is the goal. This will also allow us to leave an inheritance for our children's children which the bible admonishes us to do.

Another way to create passive income is by participating in the Foreign Exchange Market, which happens to be a 5.3 trillion dollar a day industry. By sharing both opportunities I have been able to save and invest while making a passive income. By creating multiple streams of income, this allows us to create cash flow that can begin paying off debts. Once the debts have been tackled, then saving and investing will be possible.

Pouring into our children is one of the most important investments that we could ever make. I see organizations that are starting non-profit organizations that teaches children about money and how to trade, which is phenomenal. This generation is hungry for success, and even as an educator, I must admit that the schools aren't preparing our children to be successful in the financial arena. They are being introduced to debt before they can even get out of college. These are the areas where we need interventions. We need to plant seeds early on in our children so that they can resist the desire to become involved in the fiat system of debt.

I've been working with my youngest son, since he's the last one at home with me. He has a great understanding of money, and he's already decided that he's not going to get into debt not even to buy a house or car. He already knows he's going to be a multi-millionaire, and I place him in that environment and model for him every opportunity I get. He understands how money is supposed to work for him, and he's not supposed to be toiling trying to make ends meet.

Once we began empowering each other financially, in turn our communities will be turned around, and we can prevent misfortune in the lives of others. We can move away from the selfish mentality that has prevented the world from being a kingdom of heaven on earth, once we accept that God want us to be rich for the sake of the kingdom and embrace the fact that Jesus has already done everything that he's going to do because he's seating at the right hand of God. We can no longer give the religious answers about how we are still waiting on the Lord, MESSAGE!!!-He's waiting on YOU! We can no longer frown on people because they own airplanes, mansions, and corporations because they were obedient to the will of God. We all serve the same God, and his not a respecter of person, but he is a respecter of faith. It's time to P.O.P. (Prosper on Purpose).

Don't wait another minute, LET" S GO!!

Notes/Reflection

ABOUT THE AUTHOR

Anastasia Means Dallas is an Author, Educator, and Wealthbuilder who is passionate about seeing people win in every area of their life. Having faced many difficulties in life, she has learned how to turn her pain into passion by helping others triumph. She is the proud wife of Roy Dallas Jr., and the mother of three Kings: Cameron, Jalen, and Zachary.

She was born in Hartford, Connecticut, but she was reared mostly in Tallahassee, Florida. She's a proud graduate of Florida A & M University, (B.S.) and Nova Southeastern University (M.A.). She currently lives abroad, and she enjoys teaching children and learning new cultures. She also enjoys helping people at church and in the community.

Anastasia introduces people to multiple streams of income through Financial Empowerment Groups, and guides them into finding their passion by first helping them locate where they're at, and then helps create an action plan to follow.

Through faith and prayer, she is living her life with purpose and on purpose. Prosper on Purpose is her third book, and she's excited to share this book with the nations. She knows that when people read it, their lives will be changed. She wants to leave a legacy for her children and her grandchildren, all while being a blessing to others until all families are the earth are blessed according to Genesis 12:3.

Facebook: Wealthbuilder Anastasia Means-Dallas
Twitter and Instagram: Adalltheauthor

References:
Kyiosaki, Robert, *Rich Dad, Poor Dad,* Plata Publishing, copyright, 1997, 2011, 2017.
King James Version of the Bible (KJV)

Disclaimer: This book is designed to solely provide information on the topic contained in this book. It is sold with the understanding that the author is not engaged in rendering any legal, financial or other professional advice. The author is held harmless from any liability that is incurred from the use and application of the content in this book.

www.ingramcontent.com/pod-product-compliance
Lightning Source LLC
Chambersburg PA
CBHW021507210526
45463CB00002B/935